D1399104

Roberto Clemente

by Mary Olmstead

Raintree

Chicago, Illinois

© 2005 Raintree
Published by Raintree, a division of Reed Elsevier, Inc.
Chicago, Illinois
Customer Service: 888-363-4266
Visit our website at www.raintreelibrary.com

All rights reserved. No part of this book may be
reproduced or transmitted in any form or by any means,
electronic or mechanical, including photocopying,
recording, taping, or any information storage and
retrieval system, without permission in writing from
the publisher.

For information, address the publisher
Raintree, 100 N. LaSalle, Suite 1200, Chicago, IL 60602

Photo research by Alan Gottlieb
Printed and bound in China by South China
      Printing Co. Ltd.

09 08 07 06 05
10 9 8 7 6 5 4 3 2 1

Library of Congress Cataloging-in-Publication Data

Olmstead, Mary.
   Roberto Clemente / Mary Olmstead.
      v. cm. -- (Hispanic-American biographies)
   Includes bibliographical references and index.
   Contents: Born to play ball -- A ticket out -- On the big
leagues --
Hard at work -- The will to win -- Most valuable player --
The final
inning.
   ISBN 1-4109-0711-2 (lib. bdg.) -- ISBN 1-4109-0917-4
(pbk.)
   1. Clemente, Roberto, 1934-1972--Juvenile literature.
2. Baseball
players--Puerto Rico--Biography--Juvenile literature. [1.
Clemente,
Roberto, 1934-1972. 2. Baseball players. 3. Puerto
Ricans--Biography.]
   I. Title.
   GV865.C45O45 2004
   796.357'092--dc22

                              2003017312

Acknowledgments
The publisher would like to thank the following for
permission to reproduce photographs:
pp. 4, 30, 52, 56 AP Wide World Photo; pp. 6, 14, 35,
37, 38, 46 Bettmann/Corbis ; p. 8 Corbis; p. 11 Library
of Congress; pp. 17, 54 National Baseball Hall of Fame
Library, Cooperstown, NY; p. 22 Hulton Archive/Getty
Images; p. 41 NBLA

Cover photograph by Bettmann/Corbis

Every effort has been made to contact copyright holders
of any material reproduced in this book. Any omissions
will be rectified in subsequent printings if notice is given
to the publisher.

Some words are shown in bold,
like this. You can find out
what they mean by looking in
the glossary.

Contents

This is a photo of the Pittsburgh Pirates' Roberto Clemente in 1972.

Introduction

Roberto Clemente was a famous Puerto Rican baseball player known for his dedication to the game. When he was very little, all Roberto wanted to do was play baseball. As he grew older, his playing kept getting better. The young boy could hit nearly any ball that was pitched to him. People soon began to take notice of Roberto's talent. In high school, he played baseball and ran for the school track and field team. After high school, Roberto began to play league ball.

Why was Roberto so special? He was not the greatest player in the history of baseball. He was not even the best player of his time, although his accomplishments take up a lot of space in the baseball record books.

Roberto was special, in part, because of the skill and determination he brought to the game. Roberto put tremendous effort into his playing. But Roberto was also special because of his sense of self-respect and the respect he showed for others.

This photograph shows Roberto Clemente at bat in a 1972 game against the Montreal Expos.

Roberto loved his fans and showed his appreciation by taking time to sign autographs for them. The fans, in turn, loved him. Roberto encouraged children to get involved in sports and gladly volunteered his time to work with them. He did his very best, and he was proud of his achievements. In short, he was a very well-liked man who made a difference in the lives of many people.

When Roberto first came to the United States to play baseball, there were very few non-white players. Roberto refused to accept being treated badly because of his dark skin. He demanded respect as a person. Because of pioneers like Roberto Clemente, the sport of baseball is open to players of all nationalities and ethnic groups. In 2004, one quarter of professional baseball players were Hispanic, more than double the number of players just ten years earlier.

In His Own Words

Roberto's unselfish actions set a good example for others. He spent hours coaching young children and teens. He told them they had to do two things to be great baseball players. They must work on the basics of the game, and they must be good people. He told them:

"You should learn the fundamentals. Work on them. Keep out of trouble. Don't do anything your dear ones will be ashamed of. This is a great game. It can do a lot for you, but only if you give it all you can. Now, go and hit one for me."

This is a photo of a poor village in Puerto Rico in the early 1900s. Many people did not have good living conditions in Puerto Rico at the time.

Chapter 1:
Born to Play Ball

Roberto Clemente was born on the island of Puerto Rico in San Antón, a rural area near the town of Carolina. He was born to Melchor and Luisa Clemente on August 18, 1934. Roberto was the youngest of their five children. He had three brothers—Matino, Andres, and Osvaldo—and a sister named Ana Iris. Ana Iris died in an accident when she was only five years old.

Roberto also had two stepbrothers named Luis and Oquendo and a stepsister named Rosa María. They were his mother's children from an earlier marriage. After her first husband died, Luisa met Roberto's father and married him. Roberto's stepsister Rosa nicknamed him "Momen" when he was very young. This word did not have any meaning, but the name remained with him.

Today, San Antón is a busy industrial area, but when Roberto was growing up, it was a poor, rural neighborhood surrounded by sugarcane fields. The people of San Antón lived simply. Life was sometimes hard. Many children died of disease because good medical care was not always available. Most homes lacked indoor plumbing. People did not always have enough to eat.

Life was especially hard during World War II (1939–1945). There were food shortages because of the war. German submarines hid in the Caribbean Sea and sank ships bringing food to Puerto Rico.

Roberto's family did not have much money, but they were not as poor as many people in San Antón. Roberto's father—who was already 54 when Roberto was born—worked at a nearby sugarcane farm. Roberto's father also made deliveries for a local construction company with his truck.

Roberto's mother Luisa worked at a number of jobs over the years to help the family. She once worked doing laundry for other people. One of her other jobs was to rise at one in the morning to make lunches for people who worked on the sugarcane farm.

Puerto Rico's Role in World War II

Puerto Rico and Germany were enemies during the war because of Puerto Rico's close ties to the United States. Since the United States fought Germany during World War II, Germany became the enemy of Puerto Rico as well. Young men from the island fought in the war to support the United States.

Harvesting Sugarcane

Sugarcane is a plant that grows well in the climate of Puerto Rico. Sugarcane grows in tall stalks that reach up to ten to fifteen feet (three to five meters) high. At the top of the stalk are silky, white flowers. The plant is made into white sugar. It is a hard job to harvest sugarcane, which is done by cutting the stalks.

When Melchor Clemente was a boss in the sugarcane fields, he watched over the men who cut the cane. From sunrise to sunset, workers walking closely together cut row after row of cane with their machetes—curved knives with sharp blades that are three to four feet (one meter) long. They cut stalks close to the ground to harvest as much of the crop as possible. The work was hard on the back and arms because workers stooped over for hours at a time, swinging their machetes. If a worker lost his footing, other workers—bent forward to make their cuts—might be cut.

The weather is often very hot in Puerto Rico. Cane cutters wore heavy clothing and work boots to protect themselves from the sticky stalks left over from the previous year's harvest.

A Loving Family

The Clementes taught their children to be good people. They stressed education, hard work, and respect for others. Roberto's mother took him to church, which gave him strong values. Those values and his family's love would help Roberto cope later when he faced problems in the United States.

Melchor Clemente taught his son to have self-respect because the family came from a proud people—the Jíbaros. The Jíbaros were descended from the Taíno Indians, the first people to live in Puerto Rico. Known for their independence, the Jíbaros are creators of the island's musical traditions. Melchor told his son that he must work hard, be honest, and share with those who have less. This path of self-respect and pride, he explained, was the way of the Jíbaros.

Roberto respected and appreciated his parents. He often asked his mother for *la bendición,* a Spanish word for "blessing." This was a traditional way of showing respect to a parent or older person. Matino said of his little brother, "Roberto was a good kid. He never got into trouble. He played ball and stayed home."

During the war, when food was scarce, Roberto's parents fed the children first. They ate what was left over. After dinner, the family spent the evenings laughing and telling jokes. Roberto would say that there was never any hate in the house.

Baseball Fever

Roberto started playing baseball before he was old enough for school. His older brothers played ball and he wanted to be just like them. Roberto and other boys could not buy much real baseball equipment. They often made their own. They knotted rags together or used old tin cans as balls. They used tree branches as bats. Old coffee sacks became gloves or bases.

Roberto bought rubber balls very often. He squeezed them for hours to build strength in his throwing arm, hands, and fingers. He also practiced catching. He would throw the rubber ball against a wall. In bed, he would throw it against the ceiling. He and a friend would throw a ball back and forth as they walked to school.

Sometimes Roberto played until it was dark. He would get in trouble for coming home hours after dinner. One day when he missed dinner, his mother Luisa decided to punish Roberto. She started to burn his bat, but Roberto pulled it out of the fire and saved it. He asked his mother to forgive him for being late to dinner. Luisa felt bad and later apologized.

Even as a child, Roberto sensed that his purpose in life was to become a professional ball player. His mother hoped that he would become an engineer and build roads and bridges. These were things Puerto Rico needed. Yet as she watched Roberto, Luisa came to believe that he might have a different purpose.

Jackie Robinson was the first African American to play in the major leagues. This photo is from 1953.

Chapter 2:
A Ticket Out

Roberto admired his father and loved to go to work with him. Melchor Clemente was a hard worker who had more than one job. He taught his son that people must work for what they want. Roberto learned. When he was nine, he wanted a bicycle. To earn the money, he rose at six in the morning to fetch milk for a neighbor. He carried a metal milk can 0.5 miles (0.8 kilometers) to the general store and filled it. Then he would drag the heavy can all the way back. He earned a few pennies a day for this. It took him three years, but he finally earned enough money to buy a used bicycle.

Winter Leagues

Many professional baseball players play during winter to stay in shape. After the regular season ends, they go to Puerto Rico to play in the Puerto Rican winter leagues.

Baseball was a **segregated** sport in the United States until 1947. Segregation is forced separation of the races. Players of different races were not allowed to play on the same team, or in the same league. They could not use the same hotels, restaurants, or drinking fountains. But in Puerto Rico, everyone played together, including players from the United States Negro Leagues. Those were the leagues for African-American players.

Roberto's favorite Negro League player was Monte Irvin, an outfielder for the New York Giants. Irvin played for the San Juan Senadores (Spanish for "Senators") in the winter leagues.

Sometimes Roberto's father sent him into Puerto Rico's capital, San Juan, on an errand. Sometimes Roberto stayed to watch a game. He watched Monte Irvin play several times. Irvin noticed the shy young Puerto Rican boy who kept returning to watch him play. Over time, the two developed a friendship. Irvin let Roberto carry his glove for him. Sometimes he gave Roberto baseballs to keep.

Roberto's Style

Roberto played on his first neighborhood baseball team when he was eight. His father watched his son hit ten home runs in a game one day. That was when he realized how good Roberto was. Six years later, fourteen-year-old Roberto and his friends were still playing sandlot ball. They were still using a stick for a bat and old tin cans for baseballs. A man named Roberto Marín drove by. He was **scouting** the area to find good ballplayers to play on a softball team sponsored by a rice company, Sello Rojo.

This is a picture of Monte Irvin throwing. Clemente learned from Irvin.

Marín noticed Roberto right away. There were tin cans all over the field that Roberto had hit. He told Roberto to go to the nearby town of Carolina to try out for the softball team. Soon, Roberto Clemente was wearing the red-and-white T-shirt of the Sello Rojo team—his first uniform. At first he played shortstop because he had a strong arm. Later, Marín moved him to the outfield. Roberto became known for his amazing catches and for his long hits to right field. The fans loved his all-out style of play. His cap would fall off because he played so hard.

Roberto still spent every hour he could playing ball, either for the Sello Rojo team or just with his friends. He continued to carry a rubber ball to squeeze on. Marín described Roberto as "a complete athlete. He had a strong arm and speed." It was not long before Roberto caught the attention of local baseball leagues.

High School Years

In 1950, 16-year-old Roberto not only played softball for Sello Rojo but he was also on two baseball teams. He played for the Juncos in the Puerto Rican Double-A League. This was a big step because the level of play matched that of some professional **minor leagues.** Roberto also played shortstop on his high school baseball team.

Roberto worked hard to become a great all-around athlete. He joined the track and field team and performed as well as he did in baseball. He triple-jumped 45 feet (15 meters), an outstanding distance, and high-jumped 6 feet (2 meters). Triple jumpers jump from a running start that combines a hop, skip, and a jump. High jumpers jump for height over a **horizontal** bar.

Roberto's teammates saw his talent. Once, they had to talk Roberto into entering a race in an important track meet. Roberto did not think he was fast enough to beat the other team's runner, who was the best high school runner in Puerto Rico. It was a close race, but Roberto managed to win.

Roberto's favorite event in track and field was the javelin throw. A javelin is a light spear that is thrown for distance. Roberto once threw the javelin 195 feet (64 meters), which is very far for a high school athlete. Many people thought Roberto would be Puerto Rico's Olympic candidate in track and field for the 1952 Olympic Games. But Roberto was not interested. He just wanted to play baseball.

Spotted by the Big Leagues

Roberto Marín continued to be amazed by Roberto. He thought Roberto was good enough to play professionally. In 1952, when Roberto was still in high school, Marín introduced him to Pedrín Zorilla, the owner of a winter league team called the Santurce Cangrejeros. The team combined Hispanic-American players from the United States Negro Leagues and Hispanic ballplayers from Latin America. The Cangrejeros were considered a strong team.

When Zorilla formed his team in 1939, baseball was still **segregated.** It stayed segregated until the Brooklyn Dodgers signed the African-American player Jackie Robinson in 1947. Zorilla also **scouted** for American **major league** teams. He helped players develop their skills in Puerto Rico. Then he helped them get a contract with American major league teams.

Zorilla invited Roberto and 72 others to a tryout for the chief scout in Latin America for the Dodgers. The players lined up in center field to throw the ball to home plate. Throws went a little too wide of the plate or too high or not fast enough. But Roberto's throw was lightning fast right over home plate. The **scout** told him to do it again. Once more Roberto's ball flew fast and straight to land with a loud smack in the catcher's mitt.

In the 60-yard (55-meter) dash, Roberto flew past the others to finish in 6.4 seconds. The world record was 6.1 seconds. The scout yelled, *"Uno más"* (Spanish for "Once more"). Again Roberto's time was 6.4 seconds.

The tryout ended for the other players. Roberto continued, batting alone. The scout watched as Roberto kept hitting line drives to the right and ground balls up the middle. Roberto was the best natural athlete he had ever seen. He thought the Dodgers should sign him. But there was a rule that prevented the scout from signing seventeen-year-old Roberto. Players could not be signed to a United States **major league** baseball team until they were eighteen.

The Santurce Cangrejeros

Puerto Rican teams did not have that rule. Pedrín Zorilla signed Roberto to a contract for $400. Roberto was then paid $40 a week to play for the Santurce Cangrejeros. This was a lot of money for playing a 10-week season in the Puerto Rican Winter League.

But Roberto did not play very often. Zorilla thought that young players should learn by watching the more experienced players. Roberto did not think so. Several times, he grew restless sitting on the bench. He threatened to quit the team. The team manager encouraged Roberto to be patient.

During the 1953–54 season, Roberto's second, he played right field. By the end of the season, scouts from the New York Giants and the Brooklyn Dodgers wanted to sign Roberto. The Dodgers offered him a signing **bonus** of $10,000 and a $5,000 yearly salary. This was a lot of money. He accepted their offer with a handshake.

A few days later, the Milwaukee Braves offered even more: a $28,000 signing bonus! Roberto asked his mother what to do. She replied, "If you gave your word to one team, then you must keep your word." Roberto agreed.

Clemente played in 1954 for the Brooklyn Dodgers minor league team, the Montreal Royals. This is their stadium in a 1930s photo.

Chapter 3:
On to the Big Leagues

I n the spring of 1954, nineteen-year-old Roberto left Puerto Rico. He moved, but not to live in New York, where the Brooklyn Dodgers played. Instead, he moved to Montreal, Canada, where he would play for the Montreal Royals.

The Montreal Royals were a **minor league** team owned by the Brooklyn Dodgers. Minor league teams are owned by **major league** teams, which are the best teams in the country. Major league teams often send young players to a minor league team (also called farm teams) to improve their skills for a season or two.

The Brooklyn Dodgers did not intend to let Roberto play for them during his rookie season. The Dodgers decided to send him to play in the minor leagues so he could spend his first year working on his skills. But that was not the only reason they sent Roberto to Montreal.

The other reason was that there was no room for Roberto in the Dodgers' outfield. The Dodgers had a great team with a lineup that included Jackie Robinson and other great players. With players like these in the outfield, the Dodgers had won the National League **pennant** the previous year.

The Dodgers' real reason for signing Roberto was because they did not want him to play for any other team, especially their rivals, the New York Giants. When the Dodgers' **scout** had seen how good the young ballplayer was, the team's owners decided to sign him so no one else could have him. Roberto had been taken advantage of.

A Difficult Time

For Roberto, life in Montreal was very different from life on the island of Puerto Rico. In spring there was snow on the mountain peaks around Montreal. The weather was cool even in midsummer, and the food was not like what he ate in Puerto Rico.

The languages people spoke were different, too. Roberto spoke Spanish, but in Montreal, most people speak French. Most of his teammates spoke English, but Roberto only knew a few words of that language. Only three of his teammates spoke Spanish.

Not being able to speak to other people made it very hard to make new friends. Roberto felt lonely and confused. The language differences also made everyday activities difficult. Roberto could not read a menu in a restaurant. He could not read the signs on buses and in stores.

The Montreal Royals played in the International League and traveled to other cities. The league had three teams in Canada, one team in Cuba, and four in United States cities. When the Royals traveled, Roberto had to get used to something else—**segregation.** This was a new experience for the young player from Puerto Rico.

When the Royals played in Richmond, Virginia, dark-skinned team members (both Hispanics and African American) were segregated. They could not stay in the same hotels with the white players or eat in the same restaurants. They had to drink from separate drinking fountains. Roberto was shocked. He did not realize that even though dark-skinned people were now allowed to play **major league** baseball, not everyone accepted the idea. The American South was not like Puerto Rico.

Roberto faced another challenge on the baseball field. He did not get to play every game. The opening week of the season, Roberto hit a 400-foot (135-meter) home run over the left field wall of the Royals' home stadium. He was the first player in the team's history to do that. The next day the Royals manager did not put Roberto in the game. As Roberto sat on the bench, he wondered why he did not get to play.

A week later Roberto was put in the starting lineup. During the first inning Roberto came up to bat with the bases loaded. To his amazement, he was **benched** just before he was to come to bat. A **pinch hitter** was called in. Roberto again wondered why he was not allowed to play. Several days later, Roberto made three triples in one game, only to find himself benched again. This pattern repeated itself most of the season.

A New Rule

Roberto was puzzled. He asked why he did not get to play more. He was told that it was for the best because he was a rookie. Actually, what he did not know was that the Dodgers wanted to hide him from other teams until they were ready to let him play in a few years. The reason they did not want other teams to see him was because of the league's new signing **bonus** rule.

The new signing rule was supposed to prevent the common practice of teams hiring a new player just to keep other teams from having him. The rule stated that any team paying more than a $4,000 signing bonus to a new player had to keep him with the **major league** team for the player's entire first season.

If the team sent him to a **minor league** team, such as the Montreal Royals, they risked losing the player at the end of the season. Major league teams drafted, or picked, players from the minor leagues in reverse order. The major league team that came in last got first pick of any available player that had been paid more than $4,000.

Roberto received a $10,000 bonus when he signed. Then he had not been put on the Dodgers team, but on a minor league team. That meant another major league team could sign Roberto. The Dodgers were trying their best to keep attention away from their new player so that other teams would not see what a good player Roberto was and try to draft him.

After a year the rule was changed because it did not seem to be a good rule once it was tried. It affected Roberto, though, because he was signed the only year the rule was in effect.

Spotted by a Scout

Branch Rickey was the general manager of the Pittsburgh Pirates. The Pirates had come in last in their league for the past two seasons, which meant they would get first pick of any available bonus players. Rickey sent a **scout** to watch the Montreal Royals play. The scout was very impressed by Roberto's practice throws before the game. He could barely take his eyes off him.

The scout telephoned Branch Rickey right away to tell him what a great player Roberto was. Rickey was interested, especially when he learned that Roberto could be drafted under the new rule for bonus players.

Branch Rickey, A Great Team Manager

In 1951 the Pittsburgh Pirates hired Branch Rickey to bring the team out of last place in the National League. Rickey was respected for building teams. He had a flashy personal style and was not afraid to take strong action when he felt he was right. In 1953, when popular hitter Ralph Kiner asked him for a raise, Rickey said no. "We finished last with you; we can finish last without you," he told Kiner. Pirates fans were upset when Rickey traded Kiner, and attendance fell sharply. Many of the players also disliked Rickey because he refused to raise their salaries.

Over the next four years, Rickey brought in talented young players, such as second baseman Bill Mazeroski, for the Pirates' minor and **major league** teams. Roberto Clemente was also signed with Rickey's approval.

By 1955 the team had many good, young players. But Rickey was fired after the Pirates finished last for the fourth year in a row. Three years later the players he had signed for the Pirates took second place in the league and won the **pennant.** They came in first in 1960.

Rickey wanted to be sure of Roberto's talent, so he sent another **scout** named Howie Haak to watch him play in another game. The Royals' manager knew why the scout was there. Roberto was supposed to bat, but the manager replaced him with another hitter so that Haak would not see him play.

Ready to Quit

After the game, Haak went to the hotel where the team was staying. Roberto, angry at being **benched,** was packing his bags. He was ready to go back to Puerto Rico. The scout explained to the young outfielder that if he went home now, the new rule under which he had signed his contract would prevent him from joining another team. Roberto would have to return to Montreal the following season and most likely face the same situation with the Royals next year. The Dodgers were still hoping to prevent Roberto from playing for any other team.

The scout promised Roberto that if he finished the season, the Pittsburgh Pirates would draft him the following year. There, he could play every day. Roberto was convinced. He finished out the season with the Royals. The Pirates signed him for the following season. Roberto was happy even though he was not sure where Pittsburgh was!

Roberto stretches to catch a fly ball in 1970.

Chapter 4:
Hard at Work

Before the new season started, Roberto returned to Puerto Rico. He enjoyed seeing his family and friends and playing ball. He played again for Santurce. They were great during the 1954–1955 season, especially in the outfield. Roberto played with Willie Mays and Negro League star Bob Thurman. Mays had just won the National League batting championship and the **Most Valuable Player (MVP)** Award.

Good and Bad Times

For the third year in a row, the team won the Caribbean Series. Many people think the 1954–1955 Santurce Cangrejeros were the best winter league team ever. Roberto later said that the 1971 Pittsburgh Pirates, who became World Series champions, reminded him of the 1954–1955 Cangrejeros.

Roberto was close with his Puerto Rican fans. They were proud that a Puerto Rican had become a **major leaguer.** After almost every

major league season, Roberto played winter league baseball in Puerto Rico. Fans packed the stadium for Roberto and they followed his career in the National League. It was said that every Puerto Rican was a Roberto Clemente fan.

The **off-season** was not all good. His older stepbrother Luis became ill with a brain tumor. A tumor is a lump that can be a sign of cancer. Doctors said that they could not operate on it. The family visited Luis in the hospital as often as they could.

Right before Luis died on New Year's Eve, 1954, another bad thing happened. Roberto got in a terrible car accident. Roberto was driving home and was hit by another driver. The crash injured Roberto's back and caused him pain off and on throughout the rest of his baseball career.

The car crash damaged Roberto's spine. The pain from this injury limited the amount of time Roberto could play baseball. The pain got worse when Roberto was in his mid-thirties.

Pittsburgh Pirates

The Pittsburgh Pirates lost more than one hundred games in 1952, 1953, and 1954. Shortly into the 1955 season, the Pirates' manager decided to try something. He **benched** the more experienced players and let the younger players go to bat first. Roberto got to play often. He learned a lot during his first season with the Pirates. During the first ten days of the season, he made the National League's list of top ten hitters. His throwing was even more impressive, and he was put in the outfield. For the rest of the season, Roberto played right field almost all the time.

Roberto's statistics for the entire season were not that impressive. Statistics are the numbers that give information about how well a player does. Roberto had to sit out several games. First, he missed a few games after jamming his finger against the outfield wall. Later in the season, he missed four games because he sprained his ankle. Sometimes back pain made him sit out a game.

Mr. Excitement

Roberto turned 21 during his first season. He still had a lot to learn, but Pittsburgh fans loved his style of play. He could bat with power that sent a ball flying like a rocket. They stood and cheered when he stepped to home plate, or when he ran with great speed to catch the ball in the outfield. Roberto could throw with incredible speed, too.

During one game Roberto ran for a ball that was sailing toward the fence. If it went over, it would be a three-run home run for the opposing team. With perfect timing, Roberto leaped up and reached his glove over the fence and into the bleachers. He caught the ball, ending the game.

A Bad Temper

Roberto wanted so much to succeed that he often became angry when a game was not going well. During his first season, Roberto took out his anger on the team's plastic batting helmets. He would throw his helmet on the ground, then kick and stomp on it, and smash it with his bat. He destroyed a total of 22 helmets. It was very childish. The team manager told Roberto that this behavior was not acceptable. He fined him $10 for each helmet he destroyed. Roberto was embarrassed and decided it was a waste of money to smash helmets. From then on, he worked to control his temper.

Roberto and His Fans

After a game, Roberto's teammates would hurry into the locker room. They might scribble an autograph or two quickly on fans' scorecards and then leave. Not Roberto. Unlike some of his teammates, he did not have family in Pittsburgh.

Instead, Roberto spent time with fans. He enjoyed them and often spent an hour or two after games signing autographs and talking. The fans really liked Roberto because he played hard and was friendly. This relationship continued through his career. He sent 20,000 autographed pictures a year to children and visited sick children in the hospital. He once bought dinner for a fan who had lost his job. Another time, he gave a ride home to a fan in a wheelchair. She had missed her bus waiting for him to sign an autograph.

Roberto tries to slide into home plate during a game in 1955.

Other Hurdles

Roberto did not feel welcomed in his first season. Teammates teased Roberto. Teasing new players was common in the **major leagues.** Also, older players who were not as good as before felt threatened by Roberto. When he played a lot, they played less. Roberto did not understand why he was being treated badly. Not being able to understand much English only confused him more.

Racism was a problem. Some teammates made fun of him because of his dark skin and for being Puerto Rican. This made Roberto furious. He had been taught never to hate people because of their color. "I don't believe in color. I believe in people," he said.

Newspaper reporters made fun of his accent and the mistakes he made speaking English. They would write words the way he pronounced them. When he said he did not play so good, they wrote, "I no play so gut." This is an example of the racist treatment Latin American players suffered soon after baseball became **integrated.** Roberto told reporters that if he was in the **major leagues,** they should treat him with respect like other players.

First Five Seasons

Except in the outfield, Roberto was not a remarkable player in his first five major league seasons. He only batted .300 once. (A .300 average is very good.) His biggest weakness was learning when to swing, a common problem for rookies. But his outfield play was great, and Roberto became the regular right fielder after 1955.

Some years Roberto played well, but in other years, physical pain bothered him. If people asked him how he was, he was honest and told them if his shoulder hurt or his ankle was sore. But whenever Roberto was in the lineup, he played as hard as he could.

Back pain continued to bother Roberto. It was so bad during the 1956–1957 **off-season** that he thought about retiring. Roberto decided to try playing for one more year. He would quit if the pain did not improve. In 1958, Roberto's back improved, and he played

Roberto signs autographs for some young fans in 1964.

140 games. He scored 69 runs, had 50 **Runs Batted In (RBIs),** and led the National League with 22 **assists.** With 84 wins, Pittsburgh rose to second place. Roberto decided to stay.

In 1959 the Pirates fell back to fourth place. Many teammates had injuries, including Roberto. He played only 105 games because he had surgery to remove bone chips from his elbow. They were from an accident he had in high school when throwing the javelin. Roberto now had one less injury to bother him.

Bill Mazeroski comes to home plate after hitting the home run that won the 1960 World Series.

Chapter 5:
The Will to Win

The 1960 season was great for the Pirates. The team had the best hitting and the best pitching in the National League. They won 95 games and the **pennant.** The 1960 season was also Roberto's first one where he started to show his great talent. With six years of professional playing experience, he was becoming very successful. He made big plays all season. But some big plays caused injuries. During one game, he smashed his face into a concrete wall as he leaped for the ball. His catch saved the game, but he spent five days in the hospital recovering.

On to the World Series

That year, the Pirates played the New York Yankees in the World Series. The Pirates won the first three games. The Yankees won the next three. The team that won the seventh game would be the winner. It was a very exciting game because the lead kept switching from one team to the other.

In the last inning of the game, the score was tied 9–9. Pirates player Bill Mazeroski stepped up to bat. He hit a home run and Pittsburgh won the Series. Pirates fans went crazy. It was the team's first World Series win in 35 years.

As Mazeroski headed toward home plate, his teammates gathered around to celebrate. In the clubhouse after the game, the noisy celebration continued. But Roberto put on his street clothes and went outside to enjoy the victory with Pirates fans. Crowds of people were gathered around the ballpark. Car horns honked. Roberto was happy to be among the people.

Some sportswriters wrote bad things about Roberto for not celebrating with his teammates. Other reporters defended him, though. One sportswriter said that people misunderstood why Roberto left before his teammates. Roberto was a quiet person who wanted to get away from the noise of the clubhouse.

Roberto told reporters later that he just enjoyed being with his fans. Roberto always remembered that fans spent their money to watch him play ball. "I want to be with the people who pay my salary," he said.

A Winning Trio

Three players in particular helped the Pirates to the World Series victory. The first was shortstop Dick Groat. With an average of

Pirates fans celebrate the World Series win in 1960.

.325, he was the best batter on the team. The second player was third baseman Don Hoak. He hit 16 home runs and led the team with 97 runs scored. Roberto was the third player. He also hit 16 home runs. He led the National League with 19 **assists.** He batted .314, led his team with 94 **RBIs,** and scored 89 runs.

Roberto was in Puerto Rico when he heard the news that sportswriters had named Dick Groat the **Most Valuable Player.** Roberto was happy for Groat. Don Hoak came in second in the voting, and Roberto came in eighth. Roberto was hurt and angry. He thought he should have come in higher than eighth. Several players who were not as good had come in ahead of him. The difference between Roberto's and Hoak's ranking was the most puzzling. Both hit 16 home runs, but Roberto had more **RBIs**—94 to Hoak's 79. Roberto was also a much faster runner.

Roberto was angry and hurt that he had not been given the attention he felt he deserved. He was convinced that racism was a reason. That was probably true. Many people, writers included, were not comfortable with the increasing number of minority players in **major league** ball. However, Roberto had missed eleven games that season due to injuries, while Hoak had not missed any.

Batting Title

All that winter, Roberto thought about the **MVP** vote. He made a promise that he would turn his anger towards something positive. He decided he would win next year's batting title. He began to work even harder to achieve this goal.

People noticed a change in Roberto. He was hitting the ball so often and so hard. "There's just nobody better," the Pirates' manager said of Roberto. Roberto achieved his goal. He won the 1961 batting title with a .351 average. Only two other times in his eighteen-year career did Roberto do better (with .357 in 1967 and .352 in 1970). Roberto also was more powerful in his hitting. He hit at least one home run in every National League ballpark. He led the National League in **assists** with 27 and won the Gold Glove award for right field. The Gold Glove is given to the best fielders.

Roberto flew home at the end of the 1961 season with fellow Puerto Rican Orlando Cepeda of the New York Giants. Cepeda had led the National League in home runs and in RBIs. Roberto and Cepeda were the first players from Puerto Rico to lead the major league in batting average, home runs, and RBIs.

More than 18,000 fans met them at the San Juan airport. People lined the streets from the airport to Sixto Escobar Stadium, where 5,000 more people waited to honor the two players. Fans were proud that Puerto Rican players had done so well.

More Good Years

Roberto had many triumphs between 1961 and 1966. He was voted into the All-Star Game in 1961, an exhibition game that takes place each year between the National League and the American League. Players, coaches, and managers in each league choose their best players in a vote. Roberto felt that he was finally getting the attention he deserved.

Roberto was happy during those years. People thought he was one of the best right fielders ever to have played the game. He won three National League batting titles and six Gold Gloves. He played in more All-Star Games. In 1961 Roberto hit his 1,000th base hit. He reached his 2,000th hit in 1966. It seemed there was no stopping him.

Back home during the winter of 1963, 29-year-old Roberto was in a store when he noticed a pretty girl named Vera Cristina Zabala. Friends introduced the two young people and they started dating. Vera did not know anything about baseball. She did not know that Roberto was a famous ballplayer. On November 14, 1964, the couple married.

Challenges

During the winter of 1964, Roberto played again for the San Juan Senadores. He also managed the team. Roberto did not really want to do it. He said he was too young and that the job made a person old. But the people urged him, so he agreed. He both played ball and managed the team.

Roberto did more than play ball that winter. He and Vera kept busy with family activities. He did household chores and had fun with friends. He visited children in the hospital like he did when he was in Pittsburgh.

That winter Roberto had some bad luck. First, he ate some food that made him sick. Then, as he was mowing his lawn, a rock hit the mower blade, flew up, and hit his leg. Roberto first thought the rock had just bruised his thigh. But a few weeks later, Roberto could not move his leg. Doctors found that the bruise had filled up with blood and needed to be drained. Three days later, doctors removed a blood clot in his upper thigh and found a small muscle tear. Roberto did not play for the rest of the winter.

In early spring Roberto became ill with malaria after a trip to a nearby island. Malaria is a disease carried by mosquitoes that causes headache, stomach trouble, and high fever. Roberto went back in the hospital. Malaria left him weak. He lost twenty pounds. Roberto thought about quitting baseball for a year to regain his health, but he decided against it.

A Happy Home Life

Shortly after their marriage in the winter of 1964, Vera and Roberto moved into a beautiful house in Puerto Rico. The hilltop home had views of the distant mountains, San Juan Bay, and the Atlantic Ocean. Within a few years, they had three children—Roberto Jr., Luis, and Enrique.

Roberto loved playing with his sons. He also started a few hobbies and traveled with his family. They traveled to Nicaragua and Roberto got to know to know the local people. He was interested in their lives and their concerns. Baseball was not the only important thing in his life anymore.

Clemente (second from right) and Pirates teammates pose in the dugout in 1966.

Chapter 6:
Most Valuable Player

The 1966 season was a very good one for Roberto. He worked hard to give his best to the team. Although he was a big baseball star, he still put great effort into his playing. The team began to see him as a leader. Even though Roberto did not win the batting title, he did a number of little things that people noticed. He hustled to catch easy balls or to take an extra base. This set a good example for the team. Sportswriters noticed his efforts. They gave Roberto the **Most Valuable Player** (**MVP**) Award in the National League for his hard work and leadership.

When Roberto learned he had been voted MVP, he said the award was an honor to Puerto Rico. Roberto said winning the MVP made him happy because he had set a good example that might inspire others. "Now the people feel that if I could do it, then maybe they could do it. The kids have someone to look to and to follow. That's why I like to work with kids so much."

Over the years, sportswriters came to understand Roberto a little better. They respected his hard work for the team, even if they did not always agree with his views. They grew to admire his desire to help others. Roberto used the extra attention he was getting from sportswriters to speak out about what he saw as unfair treatment. Roberto said minority ballplayers usually did not get recognized as often as other ballplayers for their achievements. Slowly sportswriters saw that this was true.

A Leader

Roberto's relationship with his teammates was much improved from his early days with the Pirates. He got along well with the younger players on the team. His English was better, so Roberto could talk to players more easily. Many of Roberto's older teammates were no longer there. The younger players looked up to Roberto. They saw him as a leader who worked hard on the field.

Roberto enjoyed being a role model for the younger players. A role model is someone others look up to. He influenced his teammates to play their best. Teammate Willie Stargell said that Roberto was a great all-around player who inspired his teammates. "Each one of us wanted to be like Roberto. He taught us to take pride in ourselves, our team, and our profession."

Getting Older

The year 1967 was Roberto's last truly great year in baseball. He hit 23 home runs and won his fourth batting title. After that season, Roberto's body started showing its age. He was 33. He had problems with his back, shoulders, and legs. He still played good ball, but there were fewer amazing catches and powerful throws.

In the winter of 1968, Roberto injured his shoulder when he fell from his porch at home in Puerto Rico. He rolled 100 feet down a steep hillside. During spring training, Roberto felt weak when he swung the bat. By mid-season his batting average had fallen to .245. He thought about quitting baseball because he was getting older and his injuries were bothering him more. Roberto felt that if he did not play his best, he was stealing the fans' money. He decided that if his shoulder did not get better by next year, he would quit.

Roberto's shoulder did improve the next year. But in a typical example of how hard Roberto played, he hurt it again when he dove to the ground to make a catch. In another game, he tore a thigh muscle when he smashed into a wall to catch a ball. Later that season, Roberto made a costly error in right field. The fans did something they had never done to Roberto. They booed him. One reporter said it took him a minute to realize what the fans were doing.

Roberto responded by tipping his hat to the crowd. The fans thought that was funny. They laughed and clapped. Roberto believed that the fans had always treated him well. They had a right to boo if they felt he had let them down with a poor play. He said he wanted to show the crowd that it was okay with him.

Still at the Top

Roberto continued to be more and more successful. He was getting paid more than $100,000 a year. That made him one of the highest paid players in the National League at that time. In 1968 a sports magazine asked **major league** general managers to vote on who they thought was the best player in the game. Roberto got more votes than any other player.

Roberto fought his health problems and continued to play well. He came close to winning his fifth batting title in 1969. The National League added more teams and it split into Eastern and Western Divisions in 1969. The Pirates finished third in the National League's Eastern Division. They were winners again.

By 1970 Roberto had his sights set on a new goal. He wanted to get his 3,000th hit. Only ten people in baseball had ever done that. Two of them, Willie Mays and Hank Aaron, had just reached that goal in 1970. Roberto thought he could, too. He needed 441 more hits. He figured he could make that goal in a few more years, as long as nothing happened to him.

Roberto played hard all season. That summer, the Pirates honored their hardest working player by holding Roberto Clemente Night at their new ballpark, Three Rivers Stadium.

As Roberto walked onto to the new field, the crowd stood up and clapped wildly. His wife and children joined him on the field. Roberto gave a speech in Spanish that was broadcast to his fans in Puerto Rico by satellite. Roberto's Latin American teammates each walked up and saluted him as Roberto fought back tears.

Roberto received many gifts and honors that night. His teammates gave him a set of silver mugs and a silver tray. More than 300,000 of his fans in Puerto Rico signed a scroll—a rolled up paper—wishing him well.

A Good Heart

Roberto thought of other people that night. A local sports organization collected donations in Roberto's name from fans to benefit the Pittsburgh Children's Hospital. Roberto made sure the $5,500 in donations went to help children whose parents could not afford medical care.

Roberto liked to make other people feel important. He arranged for several poor children to come to Pittsburgh for Roberto Clemente Night. Later, they gathered to sing songs together in Spanish.

Roberto visits with a sick child in 1961.

Roberto helped children in other ways. He agreed to film an anti-drug commercial aimed at young people, but only if it was filmed in both English and Spanish. He was remembering the people in Puerto Rico. The people who made the film did not have money to write the script in two languages. Roberto offered to translate the script into Spanish.

Roberto urged others to become active in their communities. During a speech he made at a baseball writers' dinner, Roberto encouraged people to make a difference. He told the writers his beliefs. "Any time you have the opportunity to do something for somebody who comes behind you and you don't do it," he said, "you are wasting your time on this Earth."

Another World Series

The Pirates made it to the World Series in 1971. They played the Baltimore Orioles. Millions of people watched the series on television. The Pirates won the World Series, four games to three. Roberto was named the **Most Valuable Player.** He made at least one hit in every game of the Series. His twelve hits in the Series included two home runs, a triple, and two doubles. He made more hits than anybody on either team. It was another great achievement for Roberto.

Roberto's teammate Willie Stargell said his leadership meant a lot to the team. He later described Roberto as the "finest all-around player in the **major leagues** at the time. I felt very lucky to be able to play with him."

For the second time in his life, Roberto won the Most Valuable Player Award. He accepted the award in front of many television cameras. During his speech, Roberto did something he had often done as a young boy to show his respect for his parents. He asked his parents, who were in Puerto Rico watching him on television, for their blessing—in Spanish.

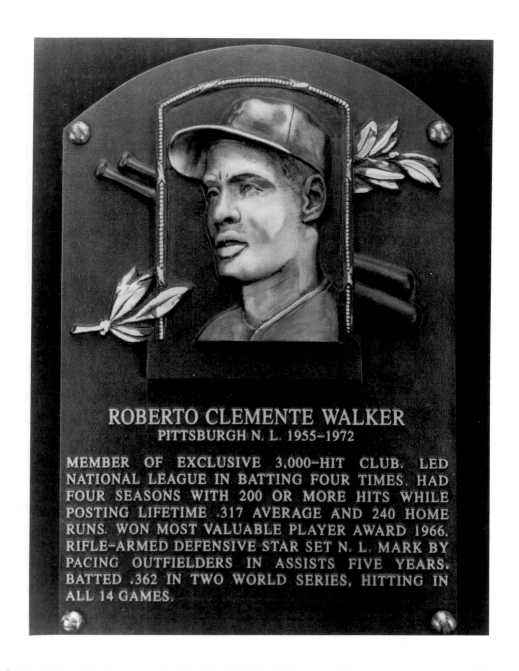

ROBERTO CLEMENTE WALKER
PITTSBURGH N. L. 1955-1972

MEMBER OF EXCLUSIVE 3,000-HIT CLUB. LED
NATIONAL LEAGUE IN BATTING FOUR TIMES. HAD
FOUR SEASONS WITH 200 OR MORE HITS WHILE
POSTING LIFETIME .317 AVERAGE AND 240 HOME
RUNS. WON MOST VALUABLE PLAYER AWARD 1966.
RIFLE-ARMED DEFENSIVE STAR SET N. L. MARK BY
PACING OUTFIELDERS IN ASSISTS FIVE YEARS.
BATTED .362 IN TWO WORLD SERIES, HITTING IN
ALL 14 GAMES.

This is Roberto's plaque at the Baseball Hall of Fame in Cooperstown, New York.

Chapter 7:
The Final Inning

Roberto was 38 years old when the Pirates started their 1972 season. He was now recognized nationally as a great ballplayer. When the season opened, Roberto had not yet reached his goal of getting his 3,000th hit. He still needed 118 more. The pressure was on, and Roberto steadily worked toward his goal. On the season's last day, September 30, Roberto got his 3,000th hit.

Roberto was standing alone in the middle of the field after he made the hit. The umpire handed Roberto the ball and congratulated him. The fans cheered and cheered while Roberto waved. Only ten other players had ever achieved that goal.

Willie Mays was one of those few players who had gotten 3,000 hits. He had played ball with Roberto one season in the winter leagues. Mays was watching the game that afternoon. He went onto the field to shake Roberto's hand.

Willie Mays (1931–)

Willie Mays was born in Westfield, Alabama, in 1931. He played semiprofessional baseball when he was sixteen years old. A year later, he played for the Birmingham Black Barons in the Negro National League. In 1950 the New York Giants signed him. He was a **minor leaguer** for two years and then moved up to the **major leagues.**

Mays was a great hitter, but he was also known for his spectacular leaping and diving catches. He joined the Army in 1952 and served for two years. In 1954 Mays led the National League in hitting with a .345 batting average and 41 home runs. The Giants won the National League **pennant** and the World Series. During the **off-season** Mays played baseball in the Puerto Rican Winter League with young Roberto Clemente. Their 1954–55 season was outstanding.

The Giants moved to San Francisco in 1958. Mays led the league in home runs in 1955, 1962, and 1964–65. In 1966 Mays became the highest paid baseball player of that time. Late in his career, Mays played mostly at first base. Mays retired in 1973. His career home run total was 660.

After the game, Roberto said that the 3,000th hit was for Pittsburgh fans and the people of Puerto Rico. A few weeks later, Roberto received a letter of congratulations from the president.

Roberto returned home to spend the holidays with his family. He relaxed and enjoyed the company of his friends and family. But on December 23, an earthquake hit Managua, Nicaragua. Thousands of people were injured and killed. Many people were left homeless. Roberto volunteered to help gather supplies and money for the earthquake victims. For the next week, he worked long hours, asking people to give whatever they could.

Roberto even worked on Christmas Day. By December 31st people had collected enough goods for the earthquake victims to fill an old airplane. The plane was supposed to take off that afternoon, but the flight was delayed. The plane had mechanical problems that had to be fixed. Finally, the plane left at nine o'clock that night with Roberto and four others. Shortly after the plane took off, it crashed into the sea. Everyone on board was killed.

Word spread quickly to Roberto's family and friends. They were shocked. Teammates in Pittsburgh were celebrating New Year's Eve when they heard the news. The next day, thousands of people gathered on the beach in Puerto Rico near where the plane had gone down.

People searched the water for days. They never found Roberto's body. The pilot's body was the only one found. A few of Roberto's possessions were found—a sock and an empty suitcase. That was all. Everything and everyone else were lost.

A Final Farewell

On January 4, 1973, funeral services were held in Puerto Rico and in Pittsburgh at the same time. The church in Carolina where Roberto had been baptized and married was full. The entire Pirates team flew down to Puerto Rico. The baseball commissioner and the Pirates' president were there, too. The governor of Puerto Rico said that they had "lost one of their great glories."

The island's beloved ballplayer was honored a few months later. On March 20, baseball writers voted Roberto Clemente the great honor of being enrolled immediately into baseball's Hall of Fame. The rule was that a player had to wait five years after playing his last game to be allowed into the Hall of Fame. By waiving the rule for Roberto, the writers were showing how much they now respected him, both as a player and as a good man.

The Pirates had a special ceremony in April. They retired Roberto's number 21. That means no other Pirates player would ever wear that number. The team gave his uniform to Roberto's wife Vera and his mother Luisa.

Roberto's Legacy

Roberto did not let other people's negative attitudes about his race or his place of birth keep him from following his dream. He demanded that people treat him with respect. He showed appreciation to the fans who came to watch him play.

Outside PNC Park, the Pirates' home stadium now, is a statue of Roberto. The city also named a bridge after him. Dozens of schools in the United States and two hospitals in Puerto Rico have also been named after him. In 1984 the United States Postal Service issued a stamp honoring Roberto.

Roberto loved working with children. One of his dreams was to help young people by encouraging them to play sports. His dream was to build a sports complex that would give young athletes a place to train. Shortly after his death, the Roberto Clemente Sports City was founded in San Juan. Today Sports City has four baseball fields, two softball fields, a Little League field, three basketball courts, four tennis courts, four volleyball courts, an Olympic-sized swimming pool, a track and field stadium, and other facilities.

Roberto was the first Hispanic American to enter in the Hall of Fame. **Major league** baseball continues to honor his memory each year with the Roberto Clemente Man of the Year Award. The award is given to a talented player who does good for his community like Roberto did.

Glossary

assist   throw by a player that gets a runner out

bench   remove from or keep out of a game

bonus   money given an athlete for signing with a team

horizontal   level or parallel to the horizon or ground

integrate   desegregate; make a group of people equal members of society

minor league   group of teams owned by major league teams; young players improve their skills here before playing for major league teams

major league   group of the country's best baseball teams; examples are the National League and the American League

Most Valuable Player (MVP)   honor voted on by sportswriters. The award is given to a player who is considered the league's best player that season.

off-season   time when an athlete is not training or competing

pennant   flag representing a championship win in a professional baseball league; also, the championship itself

pinch hitter   person that bats in the place of an established hitter in a baseball team's line up

Run Batted In (RBI)   run that scores because of a hit or a walk by a batter

scout   person who looks for new players for the major league teams; or the action of looking for a new player

segregate   set apart or separate from others; restrict members of one group or race by a policy of segregation

Roberto Clemente's Career Statistics

Year	G	AB	R	H	2B	3B	HR	RBI	SB	BA
1955	124	474	48	121	23	11	5	47	2	.255
1956	147	543	66	169	30	7	7	60	6	.311
1957	111	451	42	114	17	7	4	30	0	.253
1958	140	519	69	150	24	10	6	50	8	.289
1959	105	432	60	128	17	7	4	50	2	.296
1960	144	570	89	179	22	6	16	94	4	.314
1961	146	572	100	201	30	10	23	89	4	.351
1962	144	538	95	168	28	9	10	74	6	.312
1963	152	600	77	192	23	8	17	76	12	.320
1964	155	622	95	211	40	7	12	87	5	.339
1965	152	589	91	194	21	14	10	65	8	.329
1966	154	638	105	202	31	11	29	119	7	.317
1967	147	585	103	209	26	10	23	110	9	.357
1968	132	502	74	146	18	12	18	57	2	.291
1969	138	507	87	175	20	12	19	91	4	.345
1970	108	412	65	145	22	10	14	60	3	.352
1971	132	522	82	178	29	8	13	86	1	.341
1972	102	378	68	118	19	7	10	60	0	.312
Total	2,433	9,454	1,416	3,000	440	166	240	1,305	83	.317

How to Read Career Statistics
G = Games played; **AB** = At Bats; **R** = Runs; **H** = Hits;
2B =Doubles (two-base hits); **3B** = Triples (three-base hits); **HR** = Home Runs;
RBI = Runs Batted In; **SB** = Stolen Bases; **BA** = Batting Average

Timeline

1927: Roberto Clemente is born on August 18.

1948: Discovered by Roberto Marín.

1953: Signs his first professional contract with the Santurce Cangrejeros of the Puerto Rican League.

1954: Signed by the Brooklyn Dodgers and sent to their minor league team in Montreal, Canada. Signed by the Pittsburgh Pirates later that year.

1958: Leads all National League outfielders in assists (22) for the first of 5 seasons. Hit 3 triples in 1 game to tie major league record.

1960: Finishes eighth in MVP voting. Pirates win World Series in seven games over the New York Yankees.

1961: Gets his 1,000th career base hit and wins first batting title with .351 average. Wins first Gold Glove award and appears in first All-Star Game. Is honored for his batting title in Puerto Rico by thousands of fans along with Orlando Cepeda.

1964: Marries Vera Cristina Zabala. Wins second batting title.

1965: Catches malaria before spring training. Wins third batting title. Suffers serious injury to his thigh and has surgery.

1966: Gets 2,000th base hit.

1967: Wins fourth and final batting title with a .357 average.

1968: Seriously injures shoulder in fall.

1970: Honored at Three Rivers Stadium in Pittsburgh with Roberto Clemente Night.

1971: Bats .414 in World Series against the Baltimore Orioles and is named Series MVP.

1972: Gets his 3,000th base hit on September 30. Killed in a plane crash on New Year's Eve.

1973: Becomes the first Hispanic player to be voted into the Hall of Fame.

Further Information

Further reading

Gilbert, Thomas W. *Roberto Clemente*. New York: Chelsea House, 1991.

Walker, Paul Robert. *Pride of Puerto Rico: The Life of Roberto Clemente*. San Diego: HBJ Gulliver Books, 1988.

West, Alan. *Roberto Clemente: Baseball Legend*. Brookfield, Conn.: Millbrook Press, 1993.

Addresses

National Baseball Hall of Fame and Museum
25 Main Street
Cooperstown, NY 13326

The Roberto Clemente Foundation
320 East North Avenue
Pittsburgh, PA 15212

Roberto Clemente Sports City
G.P.O. Box 364571
San Juan, Puerto Rico 00936

Index